T0368488

St. Joseph's Table

CELEBRATING A SICILIAN TRADITION

Michael J. Longo, CEC

Compiled by Martha Longo and Grace Giadone

authorHOUSE®

AuthorHouse™
1663 Liberty Drive
Bloomington, IN 47403
www.authorhouse.com
Phone: 1 (800) 839-8640

Published by AuthorHouse 05/28/2015

ISBN: 978-1-5049-1037-8 (sc)
ISBN: 978-1-5049-1038-5 (e)

Print information available on the last page.

*Any people depicted in stock imagery provided by Thinkstock are models,
and such images are being used for illustrative purposes only.
Certain stock imagery © Thinkstock.*

This book is printed on acid-free paper.

*Because of the dynamic nature of the Internet, any web addresses or links contained in this book may have changed
since publication and may no longer be valid. The views expressed in this work are solely those of the author and do not
necessarily reflect the views of the publisher, and the publisher hereby disclaims any responsibility for them.*

Contents

Dedication

This book is compiled by the members of the Giadone family whether by birth or marriage. The women of this large close-knit family shared their talents, and dedication to St. Joseph.

We believe our first table was made by Rosalie Giadone Musso. She was the glue that held all the women of the Giadone family together and exemplified strength, devotion and hard work.

Other family members making tables in the 1940's were Aunt Jennie Ferraro Giadone and Martha San Filipe Giadone. Auntie Musso had two very talented daughters; Rosa Musso Dazio and Bessie Musso Ingo, and one daughter-in-law; Eva Giadone Musso who taught us how to make the intricate food that was to be put on the tables. All of these women were very talented and self-taught. In addition, Rosalie Giadone Musso, Selena Giadone, Grace Marascola Giadone, Jane Giadone Arduini and our Little Nana - Carmella Giadone Scalese all dedicated St. Joseph's Tables.

To these dear women we dedicate this first St. Joseph's Table Cookbook.

In Loving Memory of Grace Giadone, Martha's special cousin, friend, confidante and mentor. November 26, 1922 – November 8, 2013.

A History of St. Joseph's Table

Centuries ago a severe famine enveloped the island of Sicily which caused considerable suffering and starvation. The farm community at the time turned to St. Joseph in prayer asking for help and provision. Coming to him in prayer, the famine soon ended and in gratitude the farmers and their families honored St. Joseph by building an altar and filling it with their most prized possession: food.

The Bible is full of several accounts of men and women building an altar and dedicating food such as grain, wine, animals, and the like, to honor the Lord for his provision and help. St. Joseph is revered by people throughout the world as the Patron of peace, a happy home and charity to the poor. The old Sicilian custom of preparing a St. Joseph's table on March 19th was marked as thanksgiving for the recovery or healing of a loved one or for someone involved in an accident or during war years.

This is a book of generational learning and customs passed down from one family to another and to another again, from members of the Giadone family. Most, if not all, recipes in this book are a conglomeration of many different recipes from several of the community members in Blende and the St. Charles Mesa. What remains, after all the testing and tasting, are the formulas and recipes for each item which are truly authentic. This will give you step by step instructions and provides the reader with templates, photos, and of course recipes that are decades old if not centuries old.

Salena and Muz Giadone following WWII

From the Author

It wasn't until my family moved to Colorado in the early 1970's that I had even heard of the St. Joseph's table. St. Joseph is the Patron Saint of the Sicilian people who is honored on March 19th – St. Joseph's Day. I quickly learned how important a celebration and practice it is.

After birth it was discovered that I had lost hearing in my right ear. At 16, I learned of an operation to restore the hearing in my ear. Due to this operation, I would be honored at the following years' St. Joseph's celebration. The surgery was a success and my Nana would always tell me that I was healed because of her prayers to St. Joseph on my behalf.

In 1976 I began my career as an aspiring chef working at various clubs, hotels, and restaurants to gain experience. A few years after that I realized I had an opportunity to contribute to the preparation of the table. I would poach and decorate whole salmon or trout as well as carve tallow sculptures. I was honored to be able to contribute in this way.

I learned more about planning and preparing from these ladies in a very short time. Some of these ladies were truly artisans when it came to preparing the breads and the cakes as well as the complete feast. I was intrigued with the method and the dedication that these folks, mostly women and a few men of the Sicilian community, would come together to plan and strategize for the upcoming March tradition.

I can say with all honesty after you have read through the book you may find yourself ready to plan your own St. Joseph's Table and celebrate the tradition.
Buona Fortuna and Buono Apetito!
Good Luck and Good Eating - Michael J. Longo

Michael J. Longo, CEC is an award-winning Certified Executive Chef and the author of two cookbooks: "Let's Take a Leek: a book about a Chef, fabulous Soups, and a slightly different sense of humor," and "The St. Joseph's Table – a Sicilian Tradition." He is culinary instructor for the Mission Culinary Academy where he teaches basic fundamental skills to men and women recovering from addiction at The Springs Rescue Mission. Michael also has the privilege of being an adjunct instructor teaching culinary classes at Pikes Peak Community College.

He has had the pleasure of working at excellent culinary venues such as The Broadmoor Hotel, Glen Eyrie Conference Center; where he was instrumental in starting the wonderful Madrigal tradition, owner and operator of Nana Longo's Restaurant and First Impressions Catering.

When he is not enjoying free time with his oldest son's family; including 3 precious grandchildren, and his youngest son when they can be together, Michael is an avid fisherman, rod builder and fly tier or enjoys playing drums at church and leading worship.

Michael J. Longo

Prayers of St. Joseph

The prayer on these two pages may be said in its entirety. If a shortened version is desired, the blessing may begin with the section of prayer found later in the page.

We honor you St. Joseph on this your feast day.

We praise you husband of the Blessed Mother Mary and
father-protector of our home at Nazareth. We ask you this
day to be the patron protector of our home as well.

We commemorate your feast with this St. Joseph table, symbol of the
sustenance which you gave to the holy family. May God, the Devine Parent,
fill this bread with the richness of taste and with the delight of His grace.

As we honor you today St. Joseph, you who steadfastly trusted
that in your dreams and intuitions you were being guided by the
hand of God, may we who share this table be fed with wisdom and
insight and be nourished by a more abundant trust in God.

May this table provide us with the same gifts that you, Joseph, gave to Mary:
the gifts of strength and understanding, the gifts of compassion and love.

May we nourish and rejoice in one another as we share in this blessed table
and may it be for us a source of protection from all evil and harm, just
as you, Joseph, protected the Child Jesus from these and all dangers.

St. Joseph, you who are the patron saint of the universal
Church and of every Christian home. Watch over this our
domestic church with your persevering and loving care.

May this table created in your honor, not only be a cause of celebration, but may it also be nourishment for us throughout our life journeys.

May this table and your intercession sustain us so that at the end of our days we may be blessed with a happy death.

St. Joseph, we give you honor as we ask that the blessing of God the Father, Son, and Holy Spirit rest upon this table and remain forever.

AMEN

Commemoration of Adopted Saints

Saint Joseph

Jesus

San Giochino (Jack)

Saint Michael

Saint John

Saint Pietro

Saint Mateo

Santa Catherine

Saint Francisco

Saint Jude

Saint Christopher

Mary Mother of Jesus

Madre Santa Anna

Santa Rosalia

Madre Gracia

Saint Theresa

Saint Vincenzo

Santa Lucia

Santa Frances

Saint Patrick

Saint Luke

Let's Get Started

Here is what you'll need for your St. Joseph's Table.

The Priest - to bless the table and the feast. Confirm his availability a couple months ahead of the celebration

The Saints - Choose men and women from your family or community; people who have been ill or have suffered a life-changing physical ailment whether in life or birth to be the honored guests of the feast. You may have as many saints as you desire but it must be an uneven number to represent the members at the Last Supper.

The altar - This is a symbol of our devotion and thanksgiving to St. Joseph for helping and healing. We honor Him with this tradition: the St. Joseph's Table.

The Altar items - Various items have special significance at the table to include Breads: a large round loaf symbolizing the Crown of Thorns; a Cross representing His crucifixion; a Hand representing God's hand; the Shepherd's Staff because the Lord is our Shepherd; the Fish representing His provision during the feeding of the five thousand; a Heart which is the symbol of love. Other items to be included are Pastries, Fruit of every kind, Vegetables, Anise, Cardoons (the bleached stalks of the artichoke,) Fennel and a variety of Fish. Fresh Figs and Bone Cookies represent the Bones of the Saints. Sardines are a reminder of the saltiness of the sea. A Cake in the shape of the Bible may be inscribed with the words "St. Joseph pray for us." Another Cake on the table should be in the shape of a Lamb to represent the Lamb of God, and whatever other Cakes you desire. Candles, fresh Flowers and bowls of Wheat grown by the family are considered focal points for their obvious connection to the region in which they were planted, grown, and harvested.

Select people to build and decorate the altar.

Seek folks to donate items for the table; candles, items to make the breads, cookies, cakes and etc., as well as friends and family to help prepare the breads and cookies for the table and feast. Many families will donate candles, cakes or monetary gifts for special favor bestowed them by St. Joseph.

Contact a local florist *(making arrangements for them soon enough so you can avoid the early Easter demand)* or friend for donations of two bouquets of yellow roses and lilies.

Obtain a picture of the Holy Family for the center of the altar.

Select family members to serve the saints – an elder man. Select two family members to assist him.

The St. Joseph's Table must be completed by noon on March 18th and ready for viewing by the public. At that time, the public can take home cookies and bread provided by the family.

St. Joseph's Table by Jay Arduini-1999

Feast Day

12:00 noon on March 19th – the public viewing is over and the feast begins.

The saints are to be seated at the Head table. The table and food are blessed by the Priest. After the Saints have eaten, each will receive a box filled with a large loaf of Bread, Fruit and Pastries to take to their homes.

Serve the Saints first beginning with Spaghetti and Boiled Eggs. Rice, Fish and Vegetables will then be served followed by the Pastries.

Once the saints have been served, the community guests are served Spaghetti with a Red Sauce and Hard Boiled Eggs followed by Rice prepared with fresh Green Onions and Saffron, Fish and a Vegetable salad. Samples of the other baked goods are provided.

Pictured here at the Blessing of the Table:

Anna Marie Giadone,
Carlutta Ferraro,
Father Miller (standing,)
John Musso Sr., (unknown lady in background)
Carmella Scalese,
Aunti Mary Fatta (seated in background,) Rosa Dazio,

The Saints honored: *(Starting at left around the table)*

Tom Pamillio, Merlin Arduini, Russell MacNamara, Robert Roderick,
Pete Giadone Sr., Unknown, Rosalee Masciarotti,
Mr. MacDonald, Carlutta Ferraro

Pre-planning Guide

Grocery List

100 lbs.	Flour (High Altitude Hungarian)
2 lbs.	Yeast
75 lbs.	Sugar (granulated)
50 lbs.	Confectioners' Sugar
5 gal.	Canola Oil
12 lbs.	Crisco
2 lbs.	Lard
3 cans	Food Release Spray
1 lbs.	Baking Powder
1 box	Baking Soda
1 qt.	Vanilla Extract
1 pt.	White Vinegar
1 lbs.	Cocoa Powder
5 lbs.	Raisins
4 oz.	Cinnamon (ground)
2 oz.	Nutmeg (ground)
2 lbs.	Peanut Butter
6 lbs.	Figs (dried, Mission)
1 gal.	Marachino Cherries
4 lbs.	Semi-sweet Chocolate Chips
2 lbs.	Sweet Chocolate Bars
2 large	Krisp Rice Cereal
2 boxes	Yellow Cake mix
1 pt.	Yellow Food coloring
10 lbs.	Honey
2 lbs.	Coconut (Shredded)
1 box	Oats (Steel-cut)
2 large	Crushed Pineapple (cans)
1 oz.	Almond flavoring
1 oz.	Anise flavoring
1 C	Candy Sprinkles
3 lbs.	Walnuts (pieces)
1 can	Cream of Tartar
2 lbs.	Kosher Salt

1 C	Sesame Seeds
3 lbs.	White Rice (uncooked)
20 lbs.	Egg Spaghetti
6 each	Evaporated Milk (canned)
4 gal.	Tomato Sauce (see recipe)
1 gal.	Italian Style Dressing

Fish

2 large	Anchovies (flat, canned)
6 lbs.	Cod fish (Fresh, Fillets)
10-12 lbs.	Whole Salmon or Trout

Dairy

5 lbs.	Margarine
30 dozen	Eggs (large Grade A)
4 lbs.	Ricotta Cheese
4 gal.	Milk (Whole)

Vegetables and Fruits

Apples	Artichokes	Asparagus
Bananas	Bell Peppers	Carrots
Cardunas	Cauliflower	Cucumbers
Fava Beans	Fennel	Kumquats
Lettuce (Iceberg)	Lemons	Limes
Oranges	Parsnips	Peas
Pineapples	Pomegranates	Radishes
Spring Onions	Strawberries	Tomatoes
Wheat Berries		

Paper Goods

1 roll	Butcher's Paper	10 inch	Paper Plates
2 rolls	Waxed Paper	1/8th Fold	Dinner Napkins
2 rolls	Cling Wrap	12 oz.	Paper Cups
2 rolls	Aluminum Foil (heavy duty)	Cutlery	Disposable
12 inch	Paper Doilies		
6 inch	Paper Doilies		

Recipes

Almond Crescent Cookies

Ingredients:

½ C	Sugar (granulated)
2 C	Butter
1 ½ C	Almonds (ground)
2 tsp.	Vanilla Extract
4 C	Flour (All-purpose)
2 C	Confectioner's Sugar – for rolling cookies in

Method:

In a stainless steel bowl combine all ingredients except Confectioner's Sugar. Mix completely and roll dough out to a ½ inch thickness. Use a biscuit cutter, cut the dough into Crescent or Half-Moon shapes. Place on a greased sheet pan and bake in a 350°F oven until light brown. Remove from oven and cool slightly before rolling in Confectioner's Sugar.

Variations:

Add your own touch to the Almond cookies by adding other flavors such as: Chocolate Chips, Raisins, Dates, Dried Prunes, Cherries or Gum-Drops.

Almond Crescent Cookies

BREAD

Heart, Chalice, and Cross Bread
(not to be eaten, only for Table presentation)

Ingredients:

10 C	Flour (All-purpose)
2 tsp.	Baking Powder
1 C	Sugar (granulated)
2 C	Shortening
3 C	Water (Warm)

Fig Filling Ingredients:

4 lbs.	Dried Mission Figs
1 C	Water
1 C	Granulated Sugar

Method

For best results, prepare Fig filling a day ahead.

In a saucepan, cook Fig filling ingredients until soft. Remove from heat and cool. Place cooled Figs into a food processor and blend until smooth.

In a stainless steel mixing bowl blend all dough ingredients with a pastry blender to a pie dough consistency. Add Warm Water while mixing to form dough. Roll out to a ½ inch thickness (picture 1.)

I find it easier to take a piece of corrugated cardboard (picture 2,) covered with butcher's paper - wax side up (picture 3) and place the cut out dough shapes on cardboard (picture 4.) Spoon the Fig filling onto your shaped dough with 1/3 of the filling (picture 5.) Place ¼"dowel sticks, cut the length of your shape, for support (picture 6) on top of the filling and press into filling. Fold dough edges over the fig filling (picture 7.) Decorate with cut-out shapes for your design (picture 8.) Place the template with the cardboard support on a full size sheet pan. Be sure to cover the bottom of the cardboard with foil to prevent from burning. Brush the dough only with beaten Egg White and bake at 325° F for 30-40 minutes until bread is slightly brown.

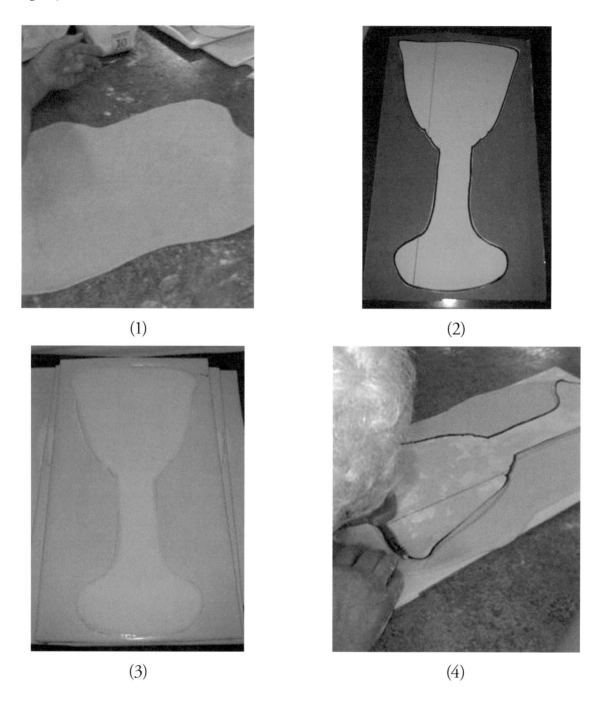

(1)

(2)

(3)

(4)

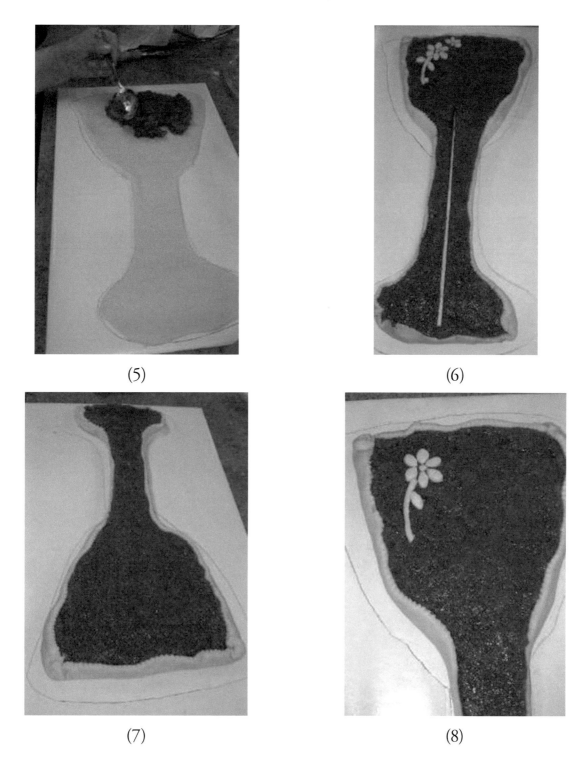

(5)

(6)

(7)

(8)

Bread Making Illustrations

For the Heart shape, use ½" dowel sticks positioned in a 'V' for support.

For the Cross shape, use ¼" dowel sticks positioned in each arm of the Cross.

St. Joseph Bread

(to be eaten)

<u>Ingredients:</u>

25 lbs.	Flour (High Altitude)
25 each	Eggs (large)
½ lb.	Baker's Yeast
1 pt.	Milk (Whole, scalded and cooled)
2 ½ T	Baking Powder
2 ½ T	Cream of Tartar
2 ½ T	Vanilla Extract
2 ½ T	Kosher Salt
1 ½ C	Sugar (granulated)
1 ½ C	Shortening (melted)
16-18 C	Water (cold)

<u>Method:</u>

In a stainless steel bowl combine Yeast and Water, pour in Sugar, Vanilla, Salt, and Melted Shortening. Sift in Flour, Baking Powder, Cream of Tartar, blending in with the former. Add Eggs and Milk. Mix completely and knead to obtain dough consistency. Cover with plastic wrap and allow dough to rise one time. Divide dough equally into round cake pans (dough should weigh 3-3.5 lbs. per pan.) Allow dough to rise again. Bake bread at 350°F. 40-45 minutes until golden brown. Remove from oven and brush with beaten egg. Let bread cool. This bread is used also for show pieces such as the Cross, Fish, Braid, Head, Moon, Shepherd's Staff, and Flowers.

Bread Styles

Rosa Musso Dazio and Bessie Ingo Musso

Cannoli Shells

Ingredients:

4 ½ C	Flour (All-purpose) (sifted)
½ C	Shortening (Crisco)
¾ C	Sugar (granulated)
1 ½ tsp.	Cinnamon (ground)
2 each	Eggs (beaten)
1 C	Coffee (cold)
1 tsp.	Kosher salt
1 qt.	Frying oil

Method:

In a stainless steel mixing bowl, combine Flour, Sugar, Cinnamon, and Salt. Add Shortening and blend with a pastry blender to achieve a pie dough consistency. Add Eggs and Coffee and mix completely. Roll the dough into a ball, cover with clear wrap and refrigerate for 30 minutes.

Remove the dough from the refrigerator and roll out into 1/8 inch thickness. Cut the dough in 4 inch strips long enough to wrap around a Cannoli tube with a slight overlap. Press the seam gently to seal, and place dough covered tube in 350° F. frying oil and fry until golden brown. Remove from the oil onto paper towel-lined sheet pan and gently tap on end of the tube to release the shell. Allow to cool completely before filling,

Cannolis

Cannoli Filling

Ingredients:

1 lb.	Ricotta cheese
1 pt.	Whipped Cream (sweetened)
2 T	Sugar (Confectioner's)
¼ C	Maraschino Cherries (chopped)
¼ C	Chocolate Shavings (semi-sweet)

Method:

Combine all ingredients in a stainless steel mixing bowl and refrigerate until use. Fill cooled shells with cooled filling and serve immediately.

Ladies making Cannolis

(Left to Right)

Rosa Faye Maurello, Martha Longo
Chris Giadone, Eva Musso

Cherry Butter Cookies

Ingredients:

2 each	Butter (sticks)
2 C	Flour
½ C	Brown sugar
1 each	Egg (Yolk and White separated)
1 tsp.	Vanilla extract
1 C	Walnuts (chopped)
1 C	Maraschino Cherries (halved)

Method:

In a stainless steel bowl combine Sugar and Butter, mix completely. Mix in Flour, Egg Yolk and Vanilla thoroughly. Form dough in half-dollar size balls. Beat Egg white until foamy. Dip formed balls in Egg white and roll in chopped Walnuts. Place on a baking sheet and into the oven at 350°F for five minutes to set. Remove from oven, place a Maraschino Cherry half in the center of the cookie, return baking sheet to oven and bake 10-15 minutes longer. Remove sheet from oven and place cookies on cooling rack. Yield about 6 dozen cookies.

Cherry Butter Cookies

Decorated Fish

Ingredients

1 each	Salmon or Trout (Poached or Baked)
1 bunch	Scallions
1 dozen	Radishes
1 small can	Black Olives (pitted)
4 each	Red Tomatoes (firm)
4 each	Eggs (Hard cooked)
1 bunch	Parsley
2 each	Lemons
1 each	Orange
2 boxes	Unflavored Gelatin

Method

Once Fish have been gutted, brush fish with Olive Oil and cook whole, head on and uncovered on a rack in a 350^0 F oven for approximately 10 minutes per pound. Remove Fish from oven and let cool completely. Cover with clear wrap and refrigerate for 24 hours.

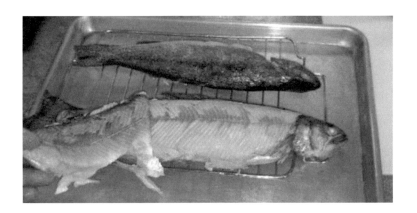

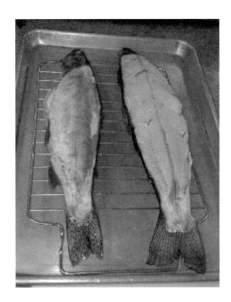

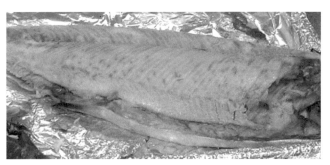

Decorated Fish (illustrations) in order

With a knife score the skin of the fish on one side so as to peel the skin from head to tail exposing the flesh.

Note: The salmon on the far right has been cooked and skinned with the blood line removed.

In comparison, the trout show the blood lines removed on only one of fish.

Removing the blood lines will provide a smoother surface for the first coating of gelatin.

The Natural eyes of the fish have been replaced with cooked egg white and black olive, shaped to fit the eye sockets.

Refrigerate the fish while you prepare the decorations. Cut out flower petals using the Radishes, cooked Egg White and Olives. (Refer to photos for floral design and use your imagination.) The Scallions are used as stems for the flowers.

Making the Fish Decorations Illustrations

Coating with Gelatin

Prepare the Gelatin as directed on box. Gelatin will firm up during the preparation of the coating so keep a warm water bath to keep gelatin fluid. The Gelatin will need to be cooled down in order to completely coat the fish on one side. Use an ice bath for this purpose.

Once coated, place fish back in refrigerator for 10 minutes to set.

While coated fish is cooling, arrange flower petals and stems so you don't spend time guessing which designs to use since you will need to work quickly.

Pull fish from refrigerator and begin dipping petals in gelatin mixture. (Remember the gelatin may need to be warmed slightly to dip the petals and you will have to work swiftly to keep the fish cold.) Build the flowers using the stems first, leaves, and then the buds and petals. When the flowers are complete, place fish back in refrigerator to set the flowers.

Salmon shown has been completely covered with the first coat of Gelatin.

Assembling the Fish Decorations Illustration

Bring fish out for final coat of gelatin and return to refrigerator. Once cooled, transfer the fish to a presentation platter of your choosing. Garnish platter with lemon and orange crowns, use the parsley for a border between the outside edges of the fish and the platter.

Finished Trout

Finished Salmon

Divinity

Ingredients:

3 C	Sugar (granulated)
¾ C	Light Corn Syrup
¾ C	Water
2 each	Egg Whites
1 pkg.	Gelatin (Cherry flavored)
½ C	Pecans (chopped)

Method:

This recipe requires a candy thermometer. In a sauce pot with a lid bring to boil, Sugar, Syrup, and Water. Cover and boil for 3 minutes. Remove the cover and reduce heat to 250° F. as indicated using the candy thermometer. Continue to cook to hard ball stage.

In a separate stainless steel bowl beat Egg Whites until they begin to set. Add powdered Gelatin and continue beating to form soft peaks. Pour hot Syrup over the Egg Whites slowly while constantly beating to remove glossy sheen. Stir in chopped Nuts and mix completely.

Place tablespoons full of divinity on waxed paper and allow Divinity to cool and set. Plate as desired and serve.

Divinity

Easter Bread

<u>*Ingredients:*</u>

25 lbs.	Flour (High Altitude)
25 each	Eggs (large)
½ lb.	Baker's Yeast
1 pt.	Milk (Whole, scalded and cooled)
2 ½ T	Baking Powder
2 ½ T	Cream of Tartar
2 ½ T	Vanilla Extract
2 ½ T	Kosher Salt
1 ½ C	Sugar (granulated)
1 ½ C	Shortening (melted)
16-18 C	Water (cold)

<u>*Method:*</u>

First boil and color eggs.

Next, in a stainless steel bowl combine Yeast and Water, pour in Sugar, Vanilla, Salt, and Melted Shortening. Sift in Flour, Baking Powder, Cream of Tartar, blending in with the former. Add Eggs and Milk. Mix completely and knead to obtain dough consistency. Cover with plastic wrap and allow dough to rise one time. Divide dough equally into round cake pans (dough should weigh 3-3.5 lbs. per pan.) Allow dough to rise again. Place boiled and colored eggs into the bread dough. Bake bread at 350°F. 40-45 minutes until golden brown. Remove from oven and brush with beaten egg. Let bread cool.

Easter Bread

Fig Cookies

St. Joseph's Table

Cookie Dough Ingredients:

12 each	Eggs (Large)
2 C	Sugar (granulated)
1 C	Shortening (Crisco) (melted)
1 C	Margarine (melted)
2C	Milk (whole)
1 tsp.	Kosher Salt
2 T	Lemon Juice
1 T	Vanilla Extract
6 tsp.	Baking Powder
8 C	Flour (All-purpose)

Fig Filling Ingredients:

4 C	Figs (Mission) (ground)
2 T	Orange Juice
1 1/3 C	Sugar (granulated)
1 ½ C	Water (hot to touch)
1 C	Dates (pitted) (ground)
1 C	Pineapple (canned, crushed)
1 C	Pecans (chopped)

Method:

In a stainless steel bowl, mix all dry ingredients. Add in the wet ingredients and mix by hand to combine completely. Prepare filling by combining all ingredients in a sauce pot. Cook on medium heat for 5-10 minutes until the mixture thickens. Remove from heat and cool completely.

To make a closed cookie (similar to a 2 crust pie)
Roll out dough to 1/8 in thickness

Dough can be cut into individual shapes of various sizes or one large sheet.

Spread one tsp. full of cooked filling in center of dough. Fold over filling. Pinch edges closed.

Other options:
Roll out dough to one large sheet about 12" round or square.
Spread filling. Roll up the dough into a tube shape and cut.

Or roll out dough to desired shape. Spread filling, lay another layer of dough, spread filling and so on. Then cut.

Bake at 350^0F for $10 - 15$ minutes.

Fig Cookies

Fruit Cookies

Ingredients:

10 C	Flour (All-purpose)
10 tsp.	Baking Powder
8 each	Eggs (beaten)
1 ¾ C	Shortening
2 C	Sugar (granulated)
1 C	Crushed Pineapple (juice included)
1 C	Pecans (chopped)
1 C	Maraschino Cherries (chopped)
2 T	Vanilla extract
1 C	Raisins

Method:

In a stainless steel bowl combine Sugar, Shortening, and Eggs. Add Flour, Baking Powder, and mix completely. Fold in fruit, extract, and nuts. Drop tablespoons full of dough on a greased sheet pan and bake at 350°F for 10-15 minutes. Remove from oven to cooling rack. Cooled cookies can be iced with a basic icing of Confectioner's Sugar, Milk, Cherry juice, and melted Butter.

Fruit Cookies

Honey Balls

Ingredients:

12 ea.	Eggs (large)
1 C	Margarine (melted)
½ tsp.	Kosher Salt
½ C	Sugar (granulated)
3 T	Baking Powder
3 tsp.	Vanilla Extract

Method:

In a stainless steel mixing bowl combine wet ingredients together. Incorporate dry ingredients in a separate bowl and then combine the two into one bowl and mix completely. Form dough into quarter-size balls and slide into 350°F Frying oil. Fry in the oil for 1-2 minutes until golden brown. Transfer to paper towel lined sheet pan to drain and cool.

Honey Glaze

2 C   Honey
1 C   Sugar (granulated)

Method:

Combine Honey and Sugar in a sauce pot over medium heat on the stovetop. Bring mixture to a boil and remove from heat. Allow to cool. Pour cooled mixture over the balls and coat completely.

Honey Balls

Honey Bubbles

Ingredients:

3 C	Flour (All-Purpose) (sifted)
1 T	Sugar (granulated)
½ tsp.	Kosher Salt
4 each	Eggs (large)
¼ C	Butter
1 qt.	Frying Oil

Method:

Cream Sugar and Butter together, add Salt, Flour, and Eggs. Mix together completely. Form dough into quarter-size balls, then drop gently slide into frying oil heated to 350°F. And fry until golden brown. Remove from oil onto paper towel-lined sheet tray to drain and cool.

Honey Syrup

<u>*Ingredients:*</u>

¾ C	Honey
1/3 C	Sugar (granulated)
1/3 C	Water
1 T	Lemon juice (fresh)

<u>*Method:*</u>

Combine all ingredients into a sauce pot and heat on low until melted. Cool slightly and then pour syrup over the cooled bubbles. Serve with your favorite hot beverage.

Lady Fingers

Ingredients:

12 each	Eggs (beaten)
¼ stick	Butter
¼ stick	Margarine
2 T	Lard
2 C	Sugar (granulated)
2 C	Milk (Whole)
12 C	Flour (All-purpose)
12 tsp.	Baking Powder
2 T	Vanilla or Almond Extract

Method:

In a stainless steel mixing bowl, combine dry ingredients. Add the Butter, Margarine, Lard, and Sugar and mix with a pastry blender until dry mix resembles pie crust. Add Milk, Eggs, and extract, and mix completely. Roll out dough to a ¼ inch thickness and cut into 3-4 inch "fingers." Place lady fingers on a greased sheet tray and place in a 375°F oven for 10-12 minutes. Remove from oven to cooling rack. When Lady Fingers are cooled, they can be iced with a basic icing of your choice.

Lady Fingers

Peanut Butter Balls

Ingredients:

1 stick	Margarine
3 C	Confectioners' Sugar
3 ½ C	Krisp Rice Cereal
2 C	Peanut Butter (Crunchy)
6 oz.	Semi-sweet Chocolate Morsels
½ oz.	Paraffin Wax

Method:

Combine all ingredients except Wax and Chocolate in a stainless steel bowl and mix completely. Chill in the refrigerator for 1 hour. Roll dough into quarter size balls and place back in the refrigerator. In a sauce pot melt Wax and Chocolate on low heat, remove from heat to trivet.

Remove Peanut Butter Balls from refrigerator and gently dip them in melted Chocolate to completely coat. Place coated balls on waxed paper to set. Refrigerate the Chocolate covered Peanut Butter Balls until service.

Peanut Butter Balls

Pizzelles

Ingredients:

6 each	Eggs (large)
1 ½ C	Sugar (granulated)
1 C	Margarine (melted)
2 T	Anise or Vanilla extract
4 tsp.	Baking Powder
3 ½ C	Flour (all-purpose)

Method:

In a stainless steel mixing bowl mix dry ingredients and then add the wet ingredients, mix thoroughly. Follow printed instructions included with purchase of a Pizzelle Chef Iron.

Yield: about 5 dozen

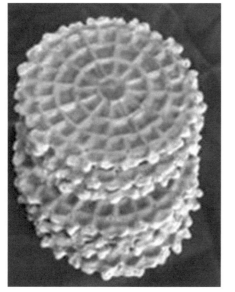 

Pizzelles

Chocolate Pizzelles

To dry mix, add ½ C Cocoa Powder, ½ C Granulated Sugar, ½ tsp Baking Powder. Omit Extract.

Pizzelle Iron
Available for under $50.00

Raisin Spice Cookies

Ingredients:

15 each	Eggs
3 ½ C	Sugar (granulated)
2 C	Shortening (melted)
1 C	Oil
2 ½-3 C	Milk (whole)
18 C	Flour (All-Purpose)
18 tsp.	Baking Powder
10 tsp.	Cinnamon (Ground)
2 tsp.	Vanilla extract
5 C	Raisins (ground)
2 C	Nuts (chopped) Pecans or Walnuts

Method:

In a stainless steel mixing bowl combine all wet ingredients and pour in all dry ingredients to mix completely. Place tablespoon size dough balls on a greased sheet pan evenly spaced and bake at 340°F for 10 to 12 minutes until set. Ice cooled cookies with icing recipe provided.

Icing recipe:

2-12 pkg.	Semi-sweet Morsels
3 lbs.	Confectioner's Sugar
¼ lbs.	Butter (unsalted)
½ -3/4 C	Milk (Whole)
1 tsp.	Cinnamon (ground)

Raisin Spice Cookies

Ribbons

Ingredients:

12 each	Eggs (medium) beaten
¼ C	Water
1 T	Baking Powder
6-8 C	Flour (High Altitude)

Method:

In a stainless steel mixing bowl, mix dry ingredients. Add water and eggs and mix together to achieve a tight dough consistency. Knead the dough until it is smooth. Roll out the dough to a 1/8 inch thickness. Use a ravioli cutter to make long thin ribbons about a ½ inch wide and 6 inches long. Deep fry in 350ºF Oil until golden brown. Remove from oil and place onto a paper towel lined sheet tray to drain and cool. Coat cooled ribbons with Honey or Confectioners' Sugar and serve.

Ribbons

Rosettes

Ingredients:

2 tsp.	Sugar (granulated)
2 each	Eggs
¼ tsp	Kosher Salt
1 tsp.	Lemon Extract
1 C	Flour (All-purpose)
1 qt.	Frying Oil

Method:

Mix all ingredients except oil. Heat oil to 350⁰F. Using the Rosette iron, dip the iron in the batter until the iron is completely coated, then dip in hot oil and fry until golden brown. Remove from oil and place on a paper towel lined tray to drain. Repeat process using all the batter is used. Ice cooled rosettes with your choice of icing.

Serbian Moon Cookies

(Similar to Almond Crescent Cookies)

Ingredients:

½ lbs.	Butter (Softened)
½ C	Confectioner's Sugar
2 ½ C	Flour (All-Purpose)
1 T	Vanilla Extract
½ C	Pecans (finely chopped)

Method:

In a stainless steel bowl combine all ingredients and mix completely. Place tablespoon size dough balls on a greased sheet pan and bake at 375°F for 12-15 minutes. Do not allow the cookies to brown. Remove cookies from oven and allow cooling slightly. Roll warm cookies in confectioner's sugar and place on a sheet pan or towel dry.

Serbian Moon Cookies

Sicilian Brownies

<u>*Ingredients:*</u>

6 C	Flour (All-Purpose)
6 tsp.	Baking Powder
1 ¾ C	Sugar (granulated)
1 C	Cocoa Powder
2 ½ C	Shortening
¼ C	Applesauce
1 C	Milk (whole)
2 C	Pecans (chopped)
5 each	Eggs (large) (beaten)
1 tsp.	Vanilla Extract
1 tsp.	Almond Extract
2 C	Chocolate Chips

<u>*Method:*</u>

In a stainless steel mixing bowl, add Flour, Baking Powder, Cocoa Powder, Sugar, and Shortening. Mix by hand like you would mix a pie crust. Add beaten Eggs, Milk, and Flavorings. Combine and mix completely. Place tablespoons full of dough onto a greased sheet pan. Bake in a preheated oven at 400 °F for 8-10 minutes. Remove baked brownies from oven and allow cooling slightly before transferring to baker's rack for icing. Once cooled, brownies can be iced using a basic icing recipe of 2 cups Confectioner's Sugar to ½ to 3/4 cup of Cocoa Powder and ½ cup of Buttermilk.

Sicilian Brownies

Skeletons

Ingredients:

2 C	Sugar (granulated)
1 C	Flour (All-Purpose)
2 tsp.	Baking Powder
1 tsp.	Cinnamon (ground)
*5-6 T	Cold water
½ tsp.	Almond extract
2 drops	Food Coloring (your choice)

Method:

In a stainless steel mixing bowl combine dry ingredients, add Extract and *water one tablespoon at a time just to moisten. Add food color and mix completely. Turn the dough down onto a Greased and Floured sheet pan. With a rolling pin, roll the dough loosely so as to not compress the dough. Place in a 250°F oven and bake to set for 15-20 minutes. Remove the pan from the oven, and allow the dough to dry for 30-45 minutes. When dried, take and break the dough into pieces or use a knife to cut shapes.

*Add more or less water as needed.

Skeletons

Spingi (Italian Donuts)

Ingredients:

2 T	Vegetable Oil
4 each	Eggs (beaten)
½ C	Sugar (granulated)
½ tsp.	Nutmeg (ground)
½ tsp.	Cinnamon (ground)
3 ½ C	Flour (All-Purpose)
3 tsp.	Baking Powder
1-1 ½ C	Milk (Whole)
1 qt.	Frying Oil

Method:

In a stainless steel mixing bowl, combine all dry ingredients. Add Oil and Eggs to dry mix and combine to mix completely. Add as much Milk as needed to achieve a Fritter Batter consistency. The dough can then be lightly spooned into 350°F frying Oil. Fry the Spingi's (Speen-gee) in oil until they are golden brown. (They will begin to float to the surface when done.) Remove from oil and place onto paper towel-lined sheet pan to drain. Roll in confectioner's Sugar or any flavoring of your choosing. Serve the Spingi's as a breakfast or snack.

Spingi (Italian Donut)

Tomato Sauce Recipe

<u>Ingredients</u>

¼ C	Olive Oil
1 T	Garlic (minced)
¼ C	Italian Herb Blend*
1- #10 Can	San Marzano Tomato Sauce
1 qt.	Filtered Water
2 T	Kosher Salt
½ T	White Pepper (ground)
2 oz.	Sugar Granulated
4 each	Bay Leaves

<u>**Method**</u>

In a heavy stainless steel sauce pot on medium heat combine oil, garlic, and herb blend. Cook while stirring to just long enough to heat the garlic without browning. Add the rest of the ingredients and stir to mix. Bring up to a slow boil and cook for 45 minutes, stirring constantly so the sauce does not scorch. Remove from pot and place in another stainless steel container and place in a hot water bath. Keep internal temperature of sauce at $170\text{-}180^0\text{F}$ for service.

Italian Herb Blend:

2 T	Basil
1 T	Oregano
1 T	Marjoram
1/2 tsp.	Red Pepper Flakes

Wafer Cookies

Ingredients:

1 C	Flour (All-purpose)
1 C	Cold Water

This is a batter recipe so mix completely to remove all lumps. This recipe also requires a special iron to cook the wafers similarly to Pizzelles.

Wafer Filling

Ingredients:

2 C	Pecans (finely chopped)
½ C	Honey
8 oz.	Semi-sweet Chocolate (Shaved)

Method:

In a sauce pot, slowly heat Honey, and Chocolate until melted. Add the chopped Pecans and mix completely. While filling is still warm, pour 2 tablespoons onto the bottom wafer and top with another wafer. Press gently to spread filling. Plate and serve with a hot beverage.

Wafer Cookies

Wine Cookies

Ingredients:

4 ½ C	Oil
2 ¼ C	Water
5 lb.	Flour (All-purpose)
1 tsp.	Kosher Salt
1 C	White Wine (dry)
1 qt.	Oil (frying only)

Method:

In a sauce pot bring Water, Oil, and Wine to a boil. Remove from heat and slowly pour into a stainless steel mixing bowl containing the Flour. Stir the ingredients with a spoon while pouring the liquid. Handle the mixed dough lightly as it will be very warm. Roll the dough out to a ¼ inch thickness. Cut dough in 1 ½ inch strips and roll gently into a cylinder shape. Fry in 350°F oil until golden brown. Remove from Oil and place on a paper towel-lined sheet tray to cool. Dip cooled cookies in Honey, plate and serve.

Wine Cookies

Table Construction

Table Construction Illustration

This table was built for Martha and Richard Longo's St. Joseph's
Table under the supervision of Joe Scalese and Ed Dominico
Decorated by Joy Scalese

Photo Memories

March 19, 1984
Presented by Carmella Scalese and Richard and Martha Longo
St. Joseph's Table in the process of being filled.

Photo of Holy FamilyTop Row:

Easter Lilies (each side), Tallow Cross Sculpture, Braided Bread, Lamb Cake
St. Joseph's Candles, Praying Hands-ceramic, Shepherd's Staff, Swan Cream Puff

2nd Row:
Flowers, Fruit, Face Bread, Baked Flowers, 3 Bread Loaves, Wheat, Fish Bread
Loaf of Bread

3rd Row:
Flowers, Fruit, Cookies
Bottom Shelf from left to right:
Assorted Cookies, Rosettes, Loaf of Bread, Wine, Cross
Loaves, Spingis, Heart Bread, Fruit and Vegetables,
Easter Bread, Cannolis, Wine Cookies, Honey Balls,
Peanut Butter Balls, and Dedication Cake

Ladies Preparing for Carmella Scalese's St. Joseph's Table

(Left to right)
Carmella Scalese, Jay Arduini, Bessie Ingo, Mary Fatta, Eva Musso

Tables of food prepared for presentation on the table and for serving guests

Pete and Grace Giadone stand in front of their St. Joseph's table, laden with symbolic foods to be shared in gratitude for favors received.--Photos by Fran Consinero

The St. Joseph's table at the Giadone's home overflows with ornate foods.

Newspaper article of Pete and Grace Giadone's St. Joseph's Table 1985

St. Joseph's table expresses gratitude

By Fran Consinero

The custom of a St. Joseph table is an ancient Sicilian tradition which immigrants brought to the United States many years ago.

In Siciliy, preparing a St. Joseph table on March 19 meant thanksgiving for the recovery or healing of a loved one, or for someone involved in an accident, or during war years, someone missing in action, and for their safe return home.

St. Joseph is revered by people throughout the world as the patron of peace, a happy home and charity to the poor.

Families devoted to St. Joseph like to extend hospitality to all who come to the family's home, Dr. S.F. Scavuzzo of Denver explained. Dr. Scavuzzo and his family have a St. Joseph's table at their home each year.

Since St. Joseph is the patron of the universal church and devotion is widespread, parishes and other ethnic origins have begun to observe the practice of the table, he continued.

Pete and Grace Giadone of St. Joseph's parish, Blende, had a table at their home this past week for the feast day.

A family who has had a member healed of an illness through the intercession of St. Joseph fixes a table in thanksgiving for answering their prayers on St. Joseph's Day, Mrs. Giadone explained.

Various items have a special significance, including figs, bone cookies (muscardini) and sardines. Bone cookies are reminiscent of the bones of the saints and sardines refer to the salt of the sea, she continued.

Sweet dough in the shape of the Bible, cross, lamb and heart are displayed and a cake inscribed with the words, "St. Joseph Pray for Us," Mrs. Giadone continued.

Candles, Easter lilies and other flowers and bowls of wheat are also represented on the table.

Most items represented on the table are breads, pastries, fish, fruits, vegetables, anise (Italian celery), artichoke, and fennel (an herb) which are found in the region. The dishes are plentiful and are arranged artistically on the table, which looks like an altar, she added.

Biscotti (cookie slices), cuccidati (fig and raisin filled cookies), pizzelles and rosettes are some Italian cookies represented on the table.

An original custom, Dr. Scavuzzo explained, was to extend the dining room table to its full length and move it against a wall. A statue of St. Joseph was put on the table and the table became a shrine, surrounded by candles and flowers.

Preparation involving many friends and relatives starts about two weeks prior to the feast day, Mrs. Giadone said.

The food is prepared by interested people at the home of the family having the table. It was said to be bad luck if the food was prepared at a neighbor's home then brought over, Dr. Scavuzzo explained, but the old custom has since been abolished.

Donations of food were given in the past, but today monetary contributions are given to assist in the preparations of the table, he continued. Many people donate candles, cakes or money for a special favor bestowed on them by St. Joseph.

A wide variety of pastries are baked including a cake in the shape of a lamb. The lamb represents the resurrection of Christ, Mrs. Giadone explained. The lamb is also a good luck symbol and represents the coming of spring.

Some breads are made to represent St. Joseph's face, beard, hand and staff. Other loaves in the shapes of a cross, heart, chalice, fish and Bible adorn the table as well.

When the tables first came into origin they did not include meats — but today some families have meat and some follow the original tradition and just have fish, Dr. Scavuzzo said. Wine was served in olden times, he added, but today beer is also served.

A custom of having sick people represent the apostles then came into being. The number of saints may be three or as many as 13, but usually an odd number because of the 13 at the Last Supper. Since then the numbers have increased but remained odd.

For the table at the Giadone residence, 15 saints including Baby Jesus, Saints Catherine, Joseph, Patrick, Francis, Teresa, Rosalie, Lucy, Mary, Anthony, Vincent, Peter, Jude, Michael and the Mother of Grace were represented.

"Last year at this time, my son and daughter-in-law were both ill and my husband suffered a heart attack," Mrs. Giadone said. "They are all doing fine now and my prayers were answered. That's why I had this table," she said.

At noon on March 19 the sick people representing the apostles are invited to partake of the special meal. The food is blessed by a priest before being eaten. They are served by members of the family and are given a portion of the fixed foods to taste. After they have finished, they are given a loaf of diamond shaped bread and a sample of all the pastries to take home. The remaining food is distributed among sick people who are unable to get out of their homes.

Each saint represented has a large loaf of bread which symbolizes the crown of thorns as well as fruits and pastries from the table, Mrs. Giadone said.

Giadone's St. Joseph's Table

Jay and Merlin Arduini's St. Joseph's Table in honor of Merlin Jr.

The Giadone and Musso Tribes - 1939

The Old Brick Oven on the Giadone Farm

Templates

Carefully remove or photo copy templates from the binding.
Take them to a local print shop and ask the attendant to enlarge the templates
to achieve a finished size of 21.5" long. Width may vary depending on design.

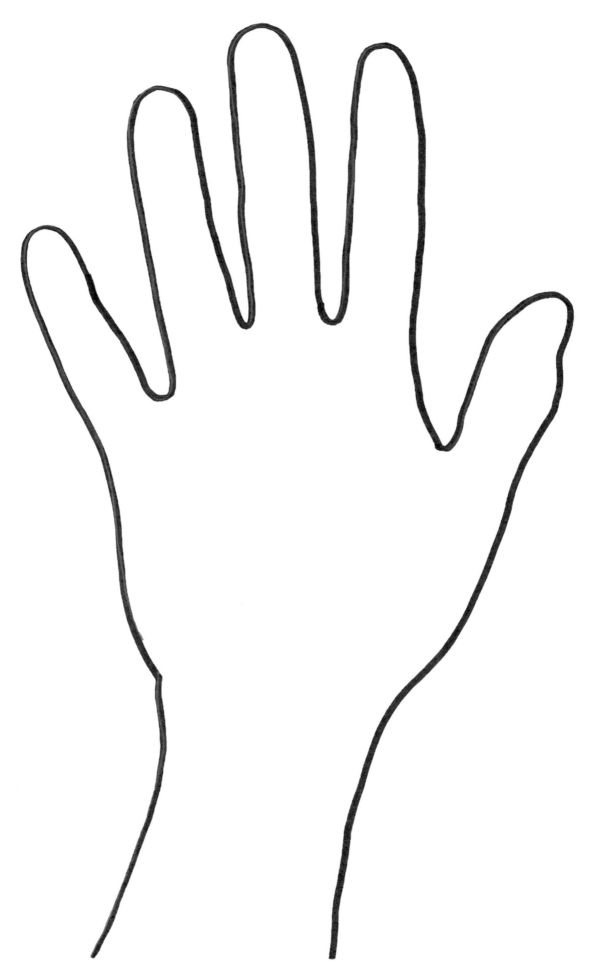

73

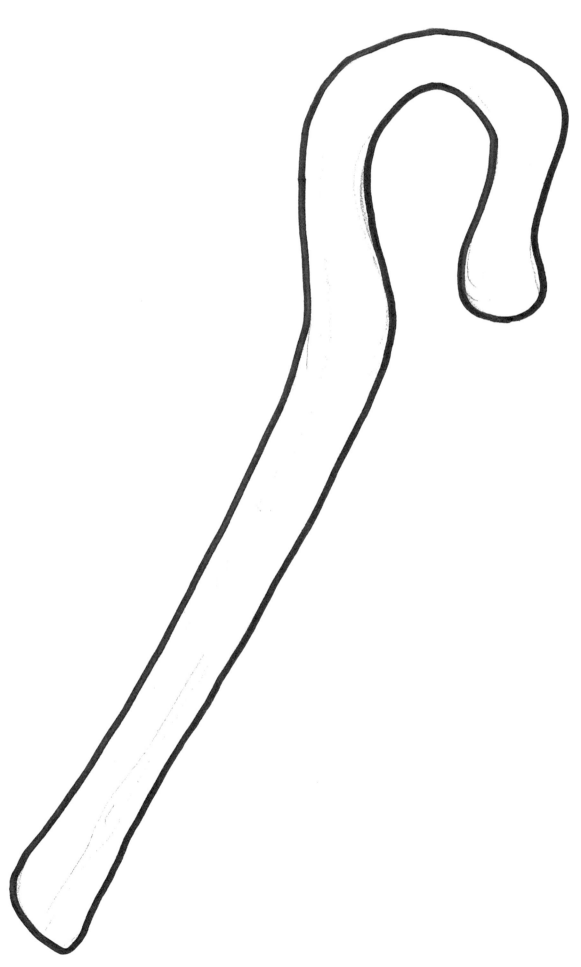

Equivalents
and
Measurements

Liquid Measures

1 cup = 8 fl. oz.

2 cups = 16 fl. oz. = 1 pint

4 cups = 32 fl. oz. = 1 qt.

4 quarts = 128 fl. oz. = 1 Gal.

Dry Measures

3 tsp = 1 T

2 T = 1/8 Cup

4 T = 1/4 Cup

5 1/3 T = 1/3 Cup

8 T = 1/2 Cup

12 T = 3/4 Cup

16 T = 1 Cup

Special thanks to the following dear people who have helped make this family book a possibility. They gave from their hearts in support of the tradition.

Marla Arduini Jones and David Arduini - photos of Jay and Merlin Arduini's table.
Merlin J Arduini Jr.: My good friend, may he rest in peace.
Richard Giadone – searching for photos of Grace and Pete Giadone's table.

Thank you to Marie Brito from Rio Rancho, New Mexico for her time and photo restoration.

Pueblo Chieftain Archives for the use of the newspaper article and photograph. Used by permission.

A very special thank you to Pamela Longo

To all the families around the world … Blessings as you keep the tradition alive!

May the grace of our Lord Jesus Christ be with you always.

Printed in the United States
By Bookmasters